A Gift For

For this child I prayed.
1 Samuel 1:27 AMP

From

STAY CLOSE LITTLE

Girl

STAY CLOSE LITTLE GIRL
Copyright © 2006 by Karen Kingsbury
ISBN-10: 0-310-81447-2
ISBN-13: 978-0-310-81447-4

Requests for information should be addressed to:
Inspirio, the gift group of Zondervan
Grand Rapids, Michigan 49530
www.inspiriogifts.com

Product Manager: Tom Dean
Design Manager: Michael J. Williams
Production Management: Matt Nolan
Design: Kirk DouPonce, DogEaredDesign.com

Printed in China
06 07 08 / 5 4 3 2 1

WORDS OF LOVE FOR DADS

STAY CLOSE LITTLE

Girl

KAREN
KINGSBURY

inspirio™

Dedicated to . . .

Donald, my prince charming,
Kelsey, my precious daughter,
Tyler, my beautiful song,
Sean, my wonder boy,
Josh, my tender tough guy,
EJ, my chosen one,
Austin, my miracle child,

And to God Almighty, the author of life,
who has—for now—blessed me with these.

*O*ne day a little girl was born into the world
and for a very small moment, her father held his breath—
because that little girl was all his and his heart
had never been so filled with joy and fear.

From her tiny hospital bed, that baby girl reached up,
took hold of her father's finger and held on tight.
And right then, that father knew he would never let her go.
Life with that little girl would always mean holding her hand.

*T*ime passed and the little girl became a one-year-old.
Her father knew something had changed
because the little girl wanted more than his finger to hold.
Now she wanted to walk with him. So he took hold of her hand,
led her across the room and daintily, very daintily, she took her first steps.
From the place where he stood beside her, that father grinned a silly grin.
But in his heart, the words went something like this:

Stay close little girl,

Be my angel little girl,

Hold onto my hand.

Stay close little girl, when you walk little girl,

I'll always be your man.

The girl grew older and for her sixth birthday
she got a princess crown. Princesses wore pink
satin and curled their hair. Her father looked at
that little princess and knew she needed a prince.
So he took hold of her hand, led her on a parade
across the living room, and proudly, very proudly,
that princess giggled at her tall prince.
From the place where he paraded beside her,
that father waved a silly scepter. But in his heart,
the words went something like this:

Stay close little girl,

Be my princess little girl,

Hold onto my hand.

Stay close little girl, when you play little girl,

I'll always be your man.

*Y*ears passed and the girl didn't want to play dress-up anymore. Instead she pulled her hair back in a ponytail and became a rough-and-tumble soccer player. Her father knew it was a long walk from the parking lot to the practice field, even for rough-and-tumble soccer players. So he took hold of her hand, grabbed her gear, and easily, very easily she jogged with him across the grassy field. From the place where he ran beside her, that father gave a silly pep talk. But in his heart, the words went something like this:

Stay close little girl,

Be my star little girl,

Hold onto my hand.

Stay close little girl, as you run little girl,

I'll always be your man.

*S*eventh grade came and the girl was changing.

She was growing up and she didn't like

princess crowns or soccer balls. Now she liked to shop.

Shopping wasn't really a daddy thing,

but some nights the girl needed a new sweater or a pair of socks

and she would beg her father until he gave in and drove her to the mall.

Her father knew that parking lots could be dangerous,

so he took hold of her hand and safely, very safely they made their way

from the car to the store. From the place where he walked beside her,

that father teased a silly tease. But in his heart,

the words went something like this:

Stay close little girl,

Be my laughter little girl,

Hold onto my hand.

Stay close little girl, when you wander little girl,

I'll always be your man.

*T*wo more years passed and the girl was invited to her first dance.
Dancing was something she'd dreamed of doing,
but she wasn't sure how to dance with a boy. Her father watched
the way his big girl's eyes sparkled and he felt something strange in his heart,
but he knew that girl needed a dance partner. So he turned on the music,
took her hand, and fondly, very fondly, he twirled her around the living room.
From the place where he danced beside her, that father smiled a silly smile.
But in his heart, the words went something like this:

Stay close little girl,

Dance with me little girl,

Hold onto my hand.

Stay close little girl, though you date little girl,

I'll always be your man.

*S*eventeen came and the girl got a crush.

Crushes made that father nervous,

but the girl was still his very own, and if she was happy, he was happy.

Then one day, the girl came home in tears because the boy liked someone else.

That father knew his little girl's heart was broken, so he took her hand,

walked her to the porch swing, and gently, very gently, he made her laugh.

From the place where he swung beside her, that father joked a silly joke.

But in his heart, the words went something like this:

Stay close little girl,

Be my sweetheart little girl,

Hold onto my hand.

Stay close little girl, when you hurt little girl,

I'll always be your man.

The father blinked and six more years disappeared.
This time the girl fell in love…love so real
the boy asked her to be his bride. In the time it took to smile at her ring,
that father's heart sank to his knees, and that's where it stayed
until her wedding, because marriage meant his job was done.
He knew that the walk down the aisle would be the longest in his life,
so he took her hand, looked long into her eyes, and slowly, very slowly,
he walked his girl toward the front of the church.
From the place where he gave her away, he swallowed a lumpy swallow,
but in his heart, the words went something like this:

Here we are little girl,

Change your name little girl,

I give to him your hand.

Here we are little girl, I'll let go little girl,

And now he'll be your man.

A lifetime went by in the blink of an eye
and that father grew tired and old.
So old, he shook and trembled and had a hard time seeing his girl
and her man and their three boys. But the father knew where he was going—
and he told his girl so—when she sat by his side and started to cry.
This time, the girl took his hand, and lovingly, very lovingly
she told him the difference he'd made in her life.
From the place where that father lay, he winked a silly wink,
but in his heart, the words went something like this:

Look at us little girl,

Come full circle little girl,

Hold onto my hand.

Though I leave little girl, I'll stay close little girl.

I finally understand.

Be Safe Little Boy:
Words of Love for Moms

Format: Hardcover, Jacketed

Page Count: 48

List Price: $9.99 {CDN:$13.99}

Size: 7-3/4 x 6-1/2

ISBN: 0-310-81448-0

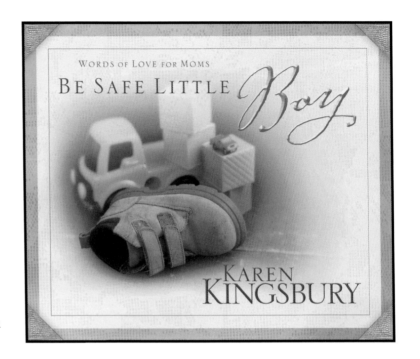

This heartwarming poem from bestselling author Karen Kingsbury focuses on the relationship between a mom and her son, from birth to adulthood, and on learning to let him go. Includes original photography featuring racially diverse moms and sons.

Even Now

Format: Softcover

Page Count: 368

List Price: $14.99 {CDN:$20.99}

Size: 5-1/2 x 8-1/2

ISBN: 0-310-24753-5

A young woman seeking answers to her heart's deep questions. A man and woman separated by lies and long years, who have never forgotten each other. With hallmark tenderness and power, Karen Kingsbury weaves a tapestry of lives, losses, love, and faith—and the miracle of resurrection.

At Inspirio, we love to hear from you—
your stories, your feedback,
and your product ideas.
Please send your comments to us
by way of email at
icares@zondervan.com
or to the address below:

inspirio

Attn: Inspirio Cares
5300 Patterson Avenue SE
Grand Rapids, MI 49530

If you would like further information
about Inspirio and the products we
create, please visit us at:
www.inspiriogifts.com

Thank you and God bless!